Alpha M
T:

How to Improve Your Communication, Social, Networking Skills, Improve Your Charisma and Talk to Anyone by Mastering the Art of Small Talk

By Alpha Male Academy, Timothy Willink

Disclaimer

Table of Contents

Introduction

Have you made an absolute fool of yourself in the presence of someone you just met? Have you tried starting what you thought was a killer conversation, only to have it die out within a few seconds with awkward silences? Did you really want to impress someone who've always admired but ended up coming across as too overbearing? If all this sounds way too familiar, you already know the relevance of social skills in today's world.

Have you observed how effortlessly some people can walk up to anyone and engage them in a bright, compelling conversation? There's no awkwardness, silent gaps, and needless conversation fillers. They are seamless in their approach and make friends wherever they go. They have a mouth like you, a pair of ears, a brain, and pretty much everything that you possess. So, what's the difference? What are they doing differently from you to draw so much attention to themselves? How come their interactions and conversations appear so natural?

Like everything else in life, social skills need practice. While possessing a gift of the gab may come naturally to so people, most of it a result of conscious training and dedicated practice. Social skills are a set of skills used by people to communicate with others in a verbal and non-verbal form. Non-verbal forms of interaction can include gestures, facial expressions, body language, and/or personal appearance.

Human beings are social creatures that feel an overpowering need to communicate ideas, feelings, thoughts, and experiences with each other. There is an increasing need for affiliation, for a sense of belonging, for being a part of a group and connecting with other like-minded folks. This is what led to the origination of languages and cultures in the first place.

Though you may not realize it at the onset, less developed social skills have huge hidden costs. Research has consistently pointed to the fact that (knowledge, social status, technical skill, etc.) individuals who are highly successful are the ones who possess well-developed social skills. They have overcome their shyness, they can make small talk comfortably, they are at ease talking amongst large groups, they know how to appear more likable, and above everything, they can negotiate things to their favor.

Even your favorite celebrities who seem to possess social skills naturally have worked hard at it. It isn't easy to narrate fun anecdotes and give killer quotes in front of the camera all the time. Think about it. It's an art that they've carefully and diligently mastered. For some speeches, public figures may have to practice weeks ahead to get it all right.

The standup comedian you admire so much takes a few months to prepare for an hour-long show, which is why he/she is so effortless on stage. The point is, very few people are simply born with polished social skills. Most have made a conscious effort after realizing the potency of social skills to master it and use it to their advantage.

The most unfortunate part about lacking social skills is no one will even tell you're lagging in the conversation department. Imagine yourself on a first date with the hot girl/guy you've always fancied. And now picture yourself unable to engage them into a fun and meaningful conversation.

Do you expect your date to tell you that they don't want to see you again because you're a sub-par conversationalist? Slim chances. Again, you screw up at a job interview and miss the position you've been vying so hard for. Do you expect your potential employers to tell you about your lack of skills in grabbing and holding their attention? Again, low chances.

This is what makes the prospect of improving your social skills tricky. No one may even tell you about your social weaknesses or worse, even you may not realize it until it's too late. It's like a small edge that can give you plentiful benefits in life if you know how to utilize it smartly. It seems like a tiny edge, but the difference in results between people who lack social skills and those who possess highly evolved social skills can be staggering.

However, the best part about social skills is that it can be easily acquired with some practice, consistent effort and mastering a few essential techniques. It's not tough to go from socially awkward to a social ninja in a few weeks if you use the right tips, make an effort to be socially likable and practice undeterred.

Thank you,

Timothy Willink

Chapter 1: 25 Big Rules for Mastering Small Talk

While some people come across as they are truly socially gifted, don't let them fool you into believing it with their confident demeanor. It's not some covert secret that they obtained from the Himalayas. They've simply mastered the fine art of making small talk. For some, it may be a highly elusive and pointless skill that people abhor, but its importance in striking rewarding conversations, especially when meeting people for the first time, cannot be undermined.

These seemingly pointless conversations are great ice-breaks that thaw the lines of discomfort and awkwardness between people. They make you come across as more likable to people, improve your rapport with people, create a flattering first impression and set the foundation for a fulfilling relationship ahead. Small talk has several big benefits. Small talk creates a favorable atmosphere that can lead to bigger conversations.

When you utilize constructive small talk in combination with carefully mastered body language, you are on your way to building lasting relationships and success. While indulging in small talk with a new acquaintance, we do nothing but trigger a common ground if interests, aspirations, and communication patterns. It gives us the potential to judge whether a person is worth our while or no. Sometimes, we know at once whether we want to pursue a relationship or no based on harmless small talk. It also makes us realize that there are many people like us or in the same situation as us and helps us take to them quickly.

According to research conducted at the University of Michigan that small talk and friendly interactions can enhance our problem-solving abilities. Several interactions involve jumping into people's minds and thinking things from their perspective, which automatically awards us the ability to think about different solutions from various angles, thus boosting our ability to solve problems strategically.

How do some people always manage to get free drinks at the bar and always make a bunch of friends when they leave? Why do we recall our interaction with some people more than others? Well, you know the answer – small talk is big.

1. When making small talk with a new acquaintance, stick to evergreen, safe, and universally known topics, especially when interacting with people from other cultures. Some evergreen topics include weather, movies, books, world news, culture, etc. Fine common grounds and interest levels and stay on those subjects. Gauge your acquaintance's reaction through body language and gestures. If they react

enthusiastically and favorably to a topic, continue with it, else change the course of the conversation. It is important to tune in to non-verbal signs.

2. Avoid centering your small talk on controversial topics such as politics, religion, terrorism, and the likes. You don't want to get into a heated debated with a new acquaintance about the merits of having a Republican President over a Democrat. Not yet. Keep conversations neutral and non-intimidating.

3. Be a good listener. Being high on social skills doesn't mean you talk non-stop. It also means you give the other person the opportunity to talk, be a good listener, and respond encouragingly. No one likes to make even small talk with a person who is zealously talking nineteen to a dozen only about himself. Make a person feel relaxed and comfortable by listening to him with interest. Acknowledge what he says through gestures and body language (bending slightly forward while speaking signals you're deeply interested in the conversation and are following whatever he's saying keenly) and suitable affirmations.

4. Centre the talk on positive things rather than unpleasant or negative ideas. Also, stick to topics that people can easily relate to or agree with. Don't come up with topics where there can be plenty of disagreements and conflicting opinions. Anything that's simple to agree with makes for a good starting point for small talk.

5. Resist the "me too" syndrome. Sometimes, in the middle of a conversation, we find ourselves relating to the exact scenario that's being narrated by the other person. The temptation to say me too and give an account of our story can be overpowering. However, in the larger interests of the conversation, it is important to let the other person finish their narration before you jump on with your tale.

6. If you want to come across as more likable to people, mirror them. Use the same words as they do. Speak in their tone and language. Try using the same gestures as they do. Echo their phrases and words. Now, don't make this like comical repeat after me process. You should be able to seamlessly mirror their actions to make them identify more with you. For instance, if you notice that they keep referring to their business as an "empire", you should also try to refer to their business as an "empire". This will increase your appeal, make your acquaintance feel more in unison with you with, and boost your likability. Once you make yourself more likable and identifiable to people, you increase your chances of responding more positively to your proposals.

7. If at any stage, you don't find yourself agreeing with what your new acquaintance said, instead of getting defensive and launching a candid attack on him to pull apart his arguments bit by bit, try a more diplomatic yet honest approach. Say something safe

like "that's a really different way of looking at it". I am intrigued. Can you elaborate on it?" This gives you the ability to show your disagreement without causing any unpleasantness.

8. Don't try too hard to be very humorous early on. People don't take too kindly to tongue in cheek remarks, witty jibes, clever jokes, and sarcastic comments from strangers. While you may not mean any harm and may only be trying to impress the other party by displaying your sparkling sense of humor, it can backfire miserably. Don't get too clever for people at start poking fun of them without knowing if they are able to take it in the right spirit. These are all good for intimate friendships when you've known people closely for years. With strangers, it may be a classic case rushing things up. Give people space and time to understand you and take your time to get to know them well before acting too familiar for comfort.

9. Avoid sharing secrets and intimate details too soon. It doesn't make you come across as too trustworthy to strangers. The general impression they will get is that you're an unethical bigmouth who cannot be trusted with secrets. Also, you don't know the person well enough to gauge how they may use the secret or intimate information you've just shared with them. To avoid any controversy, just stick to safe and universal subjects that everyone can agree with. Stay away from

the temptation of complaining excessively or badmouthing people. It makes you come across as a grumpy, untrustworthy, and malicious person, even though you may be right.

10. Always tune your senses to the finer details of the conversation. Know when you can take the talk deeper and jump at the opportunity when it arises. People will keep giving you hints throughout the conversation about their likes and dislikes. You should be able to quickly tune in to it and pick up the clues at the right places to steer the conversation in the direction you want it to go in.

11. Master the fine art of empathizing with people. This helps your likeability quotient by several notches. There is a major difference between sympathy and empathy. Unlike sympathy, empathy is not about feeling sorry for them or pitying them. It is putting yourself in their shoes and understanding what it feels to go through what they're going through. Short phrases such as "I understand why you feel this way", "I can very well understand how you feel about it" or "I realize it might have been very tough" can be highly effective in establishing a more empathetic and comfortable small talk. Don't weep buckets and pretend to be the ultimate savior when people are narrating their problems.

12. Use more "you" and less "me". Emphasize on the other person when engaged in small talk. Make him

the hero of the conversation rather than hogging all the limelight. No one likes to listen to the person talking endlessly about how wonderful they are or everything that's happening in their life or how their neighbor's cat just gave birth to a bunch of kittens. If you want to make yourself instantly likable to other people, focus on them rather than on you. Start your conversation with you and use more "you" than "me" throughout the talk. This gives people the impression about how you are more interested in knowing about them rather than waxing eloquence about yourself. Appear sincere and show that you are genuinely interested in knowing about a person. This trait can make you highly irresistible to many.

13. If you want to get people to talk more, learn to ask more open-ended questions. However, having said that doesn't make it appear like an interrogation session by an officer on duty. Ask gently and with earnest interest. For instance, if you realize that a person is very excited about an upcoming local sports club match, ask what prompted them to be a part of the club. Learn to figure out early on what people are really passionate about and build on the conversation by asking open-ended questions. If you get to know a person is deeply interested in travel, inquire about their last trip. There are good chances you'll end up striking a memorable conversation.

14. Make sure to stick to subjects you're familiar about. Even if you realize that the acquaintance, you're conversing with is a space scientist, don't flash your ignorance by getting into an animated discussion about newest trends in space research when you have no clue about them. Trying to show off knowledge to impress people when you actually have none on the subject jeopardizes your chances of a memorable interaction like few other things. You will only come across as a 'fool trying too hard to please'. If you don't know much about the subject while finding yourself in the midst of a heavy discussion surrounding it, admit straight off in a witty yet honest manner how outer space is beyond your realm of understanding as you barely manage to get any space on earth. Get the drift? Transform your weakness into an honest and likable strength. People instantly take to sharp-witted and genuine people who admit to their shortcomings without any inhibitions, rather than pretending to be something they clearly are not.

15. Use the right body language and other non-verbal communication signals to make your small talk more effective and impactful. Small things like smiling more often, making your body language more open, leaning forward, fleetingly brushing against the person's arm, maintaining eye contact throughout the conversation, nodding, keeping a distance about a couple of feet between you and the other person and keeping the energy level high (through your voice pitch and tone)

are some pro tips for using body language favorably to leave a lasting first impression.

16. Greeting people appropriately. This can be awkward, especially when you're interacting with people from other cultures. You may not know whether to kiss or not, whether to offer a peck on the cheek or simply stick to saying hello. Universally, a firm and genuine handshake is your bet best when it comes to greeting acquaintances in social situations. If you find the other person making an overture of kissing or offering you a light peck on the cheek, you can reciprocate accordingly. However, when in doubt, it's safe to stick to a smile, hello, and a firm handshake.

17. If you've read Dale Carnegie's social skills bible, "How to Win Friends and Influence People", you'll know the importance of remembering people's names. Quick introductions, unfamiliar faces and several names being passed around mean low chances of people remembering names of people they've just been introduced to. However, make a conscious effort not to be a part of this name forgetting pack. Make people feel important by appearing genuinely interested in them. Repeat their names to confirm it after you've just been introduced. This doesn't make the whole exercise look like a mere formality but shows people you sincerely want to know more about them. Keep referring to people by their names rather

than common salutations. Whether you address them by their first name or last name will depend on what is appropriate for the situation, but never shy away from addressing people by their names, even if you've just met them. It makes you all the more desirable to them. When you don't get someone's name clearly in the first instance, it's all right to ask them to repeat it for more clarity.

18. Don't panic when there are conversation lulls. Sometimes, despite making the best efforts we find ourselves in the middle of conversation dead ends. There can be awkward silences, clumsy conversation fillers, and generally a gap that's leading nowhere. You need to master the art of reviving a seemingly dead conversation. If you've picked up a few clues from the talk you've just had, you can quickly throw another topic in the air, and forget everything about making a smooth transition.

19. Do a little background homework. When you're heading to a party and are aware that you will be meeting some important folks from a specific background, try and do a little research to come up with topics to start a meaningful conversation. If you know the host or guests are a set of people who are passionate about charity or skiing or cooking, some background research about these will help you be a part of the group more seamlessly. You will know exactly what to say to make lively conversations and

bring the guests in their element. Scan newspaper headlines, read book reviews, or go through movie listings – anything that can resonate with a new group of people you are about to meet. You can be an online behavior profiler if you get a chance to know who you will be meeting ahead of time and playing Sherlock by going through their social network profiles. This helps you know their likes and dislikes well in advance to give you an edge while striking up a conversation with them.

20. Compliments work wonders. Nothing is as effective an icebreaker as a genuine, thoughtful, and well-intended compliment. Something as simple as "What a lovely bag, where did you buy it from?" can kick-start an enjoyable conversation about bag shopping and brands and can lead just about anywhere. Even if it doesn't trigger a bigger conversation, the mere fact that you've complimented a person makes you more likable to him, makes him feel good about himself and can lead to a discussion on other subjects. This simple yet powerful move can also be used to introduce yourself.

21. Reveal something interesting about yourself. Once you're on common ground, make the next move to reveal something more personal about yourself. It shouldn't be personal enough to make the other person uncomfortable though. Something like your favorite author or why you took up a certain major in

college or sports training regime. These are interesting bits of information that give a nice preview of you, without bordering on intimate details that can freak people out in the first meeting.

22. Tactfully balance questions and statements. Your small talk should be a nice mix of questions and statements. Too many questions to draw out the person will make it seem like he's being probed, while too many statements will give him fewer opportunities to speak. Sprinkle your statements with meaningful questions to give him the chance to respond to your statements and offer his take on it. Something like, "I love that television series even though several people believe it's highly overrated, do you enjoy it as well?" See what you've done there? You've let out a statement pronouncing your view about the series. However, you've also given the other person an opportunity to elaborate on it.

23. Pick up clues from your immediate surroundings. Sometimes when you have absolutely no clue what to do talk about, get help from your surroundings. Pick up clues to strike a friendly banter from what's going around you. It can be a wall poster or something the other person is wearing or something someone just said that could apply to the two of you. It could be a flyer for all you care. There are clues everywhere that you can tune in to for starting an interesting conversation.

24. Avoid making quick judgments. While it may be all too tempting to make snap judgments about people we've just met, avoid falling into the trap. We can't and mustn't judge a book by its cover. Listen carefully, look out for non-verbal clues, and understand that things may not always be what they appear to be while meeting people for the first time. Don't shut yourself from future interactions with owing to superficial outer clues. Take time to know and understand them.

25. Say a powerful and memorable goodbye. A lot of what you leave behind after your interaction with a person for the first time will depend on your parting shot. Leave a positive first impression by ending the conversation in an impactful manner. Keep it polite, meaningful, and leave the thread open to help you both pick up from where you left for the next meeting.

Chapter 2: 13 Powerful Secrets for Overcoming Social Anxiety

While meeting new people or talking to a group can send even the most confident of us in a tizzy of self-consciousness, social anxiety is far worse. It is not just about being socially shy or low on confidence around others, but about developing a deep fear or even panicking when it comes to meeting and interacting with people. Signs of social anxiety can be as extreme as a shaky voice, quick breaths, thumping heart, and sweating. You want to simply flee from the scenario that faces people.

Rather than viewing it as an opportunity to connect with people, individuals with high social anxiety are crippled by issues related to self-consciousness, extreme nervousness and being at a loss about how to strike a meaningful conversation. There is a deep desire to escape from the prospect of meeting and talking to people. However, like everything else, social anxiety can be overcome with dedication, will-power, and a few time-tested strategies. Here are some expert tips on overcoming social anxiety effectively.

1. Deep breathing helps. Take deep breaths before facing an anxiety-inducing social situation. It will be much more effective if you practice deep breathing daily. This way you don't have to focus excessively on

the breathing on specific days, and it will be more like second nature. While breathing focus on the situation ahead of you, what a wonderful person you are, what a wonderful set of people you are about to meet, and how you're going to form lasting relationships at the social do. Positive reinforcements while practicing deep breathing help prepare you for anxious situations.

2. See a therapist. If you suffer from extreme social anxiety, you might want to enlist the help of a professional behavior therapist who can work with you to help you overcome your fear of social interactions. Trained professionals can get you to understand your challenges more effectively. They can also help find more result-oriented solutions to lower your symptoms of social anxiety. Search for an expert and experienced therapist who specialize in anxiety-related disorders.

3. Make a list of exposure hierarchy. This can be one of the most effective ways of gradually overcoming your social anxiety with conscious effort and practice. An exposure hierarchy is nothing but a list of social situations in a hierarchical form, rated from the least anxiety provoking to most anxiety provoking. You start with the simplest tasks first and keep ticking situations as you overcome them. For instance, you may start with asking for directions to the nearest

coffee shop and keep going until you are confident enough to ask a person you fancy out for a date.

4. Reduce internal focus. Socially anxious folks tend to focus more on themselves than anything else around them. A lot of energy is spent in scrutinizing themselves in terms of what they are wearing and the bodily sensations (sweating, blushing, excessive shaking, etc.) they are experiencing. This further increases the level of self-consciousness. To avoid it, simply shift the focus on other people and the surroundings. Always remember, you aren't the only person in the room. There are several others who are equally drawing attention from others.

Try to focus on the conversations, other people, the environment rather than thinking deeply about your performance, appearance, attire, and behavior. Don't replay or scrutinize every line of conversation in your head to judge how you fared. Just be in the flow of the moment and concentrate on what's being said. Don't stress too much about silences. The onus of keeping the conversation going isn't on you alone. It's alright to not fill every gap of silence with pointless fillers.

5. Select a positive mantra or inspiring song. Reciting something on a loop such as a prayer, powerful lines from a poem, your favorite quotation –anything that inspires you- is great for reinforcing your belief in yourself. This can be used when you're anxious

about-facing people. These lines can equip you with confidence, bring about a feel-good aura and drive you to be more prepared to handle challenging situations. Even something as basic as, "I can talk to xyz today" or "I am going to have a stellar conversation with abc" or "it feels great to be able to meet people" can work wonders when it comes to conquering social anxiety. Positive affirmations can also be put on sticky notes around your house (mirrors, refrigerators, cabinets, etc.) to help reiterate your goals every day.

6. Alter your diet. Stimulants such as nicotine, alcohol, caffeine, etc. can increase symptoms of anxiety within the body. In extreme cases, they may actually induce anxiety attacks. Know when you should and should not consume these things. While consuming alcohol to calm down the nerves is alright in some scenarios, don't go overboard and drink excessively.

7. Communicate more assertively. There's a huge difference between being assertive, submissive and aggressive. Submissive is when you show zero regards for yourself and completely give in to the other person's opinions, beliefs, needs, thoughts, etc. Aggressive is when you're absolutely unwilling to listen to the other person, while constantly airing your views, opinions, and desires in a rather forceful manner.

Assertive is the way to go. Here, you communicate your thoughts and feelings in a manner that shows respect for yourself, without disrespecting others. When you learn to communicate more assertively and say no without any hesitation if you don't agree with something, you are a step closer to ridding yourself from social anxiety. This may not come at once but make an effort to consciously be more direct and neutral when it comes to expressing yourself. Gradually, you will develop the required confidence and learn to command presence.

8. Grow your social circle. Individuals suffering from social anxiety find fit increasingly challenging to go out and interact with unknown people. This is one of the most fundamental parts of conquering social anxiety and establishing rewarding social relationships in life. Make an effort to expand your social circle. Think of some hobby that you're passionate about. It can be riding, cycling, running, or just about anything that sparks your interest. Find a group of individuals in your neighborhood who share similar interests as you. It will be much easier to strike up a conversation with them and connect with them based on mutual interests.

Also, make it a point to attend social events that you're invited too, even if you are tempted to stay away from them. Staying away from social groups not just increases your anxiety but will also lead to feelings of isolation and depression. Even if you attend the party for some time and don't stay until the end, just go. Meeting new people will increase your social circle and give you the confidence of facing new people. You have to push yourself out of your comfort zone to lead a better life.

You can also join a class to master skills you've always wanted to pick. This way you not just acquire new skills to add to your profile, but also get introduced to and interact with new people. This acts as a great base for practicing your social skills.

9. Don't hesitate to ask family and friends for support. Reach out to your support network when you're tackling fears related to social anxiety. If you're speaking at a large event or have to attend a crucial business party or conference, get along a close buddy or relative for support. Being in close proximity to a familiar person can automatically increase your level of confidence and soothe your nerves. Turn to your family/friend if you find yourself starting to feel increasingly overwhelmed by the situation. Their pep talks and absolute belief in you can help you feel less daunted.

10. Stop thinking about how others perceive you. Avoid social anxiety and awkwardness by not thinking about what others think of you. Most people with social anxiety are always daunted by thoughts of how others perceive them. If you're constantly worried

about what the other person is thinking about you, you really won't be able to relax and enjoy a meaningful social interaction. Once you break out of the cycle of worrying yourself crazy about this, you'll find yourself meeting people in a calmer and more natural manner. Learn to distinguish between whose opinion matters and whose doesn't rather than getting worked up about being perfect for everyone.

11. Let your body language be pro-social. Don't let your body look closed during social interactions. This will only reinforce your social anxiety to others. Give out signals of openness and positivity when meeting people for the first time. Avoid crossing your arms and legs. It gives out the impression that you're an unwilling participant and disinterested in the interaction. Other signs of social anxiety include no eye contact, crossing your body, slouching, and putting down the head. Keep your body language welcoming, genuine, and open. It should be inviting enough to encourage people to approach you and strike up a conversation with you.

12. Show good etiquette. If you're not aware of the social norms and etiquettes of a group you're meeting for the first time, you'll most likely experience a higher sense of social anxiety. This is especially true when you're visiting another country or are with a group of people belonging to another culture. Make an effort to learn their norms and etiquettes so you

don't stick out like a sore thumb. Use universally acceptable positive social signals such as smiling, nodding, and saying please and thank you. People will take to you instantly if you show good manners, even if you're not completely tuned in to the local culture.

13. Participate in group therapy. Group therapy can be one of the most effective ways to get rid of social anxiety because you are subjected to Cognitive Behavior Therapy (CBT) is a controlled group setting. This can include everything from intense social behavior training to role-playing to mock interactions to videotaped conversations. The time-tested exercises gently yet efficiently help you prepare for real-world situations that make you anxious. You can also join a support group in your area. This will make you feel less isolated about the anxiety, and also let you know that you aren't alone. You will realize there are quite a few others like you in need of help when it comes to social interactions.

Chapter 3: Be the Ultimate Dating Champ with These 'Approach Your Crush' Tips

If you're the kind who feels intimidated and awkward around members of the opposite sex, especially a special someone you've been crushing on forever, fret not. Take solace in the fact that you aren't alone. There are plenty of people in the world who develop cold feet when it comes to approaching their crush for a date. You are obviously anxious about being rejected or worse (don't know which is worse for you, though) being laughed at. However, keep in mind a very basic principle that people always fail to realize. When you ask, you have some chance (even it is a tiny percentage) of success. By not asking, you are converting that small percentage of success into 0% success. You have to bear your heart and put yourself in the line of fire to get what you really want in life. Here are some brilliant tips to make your task of asking your crush out less jittery and more effortless.

1. Prepare yourself mate. Don't just go there and blabber something incomprehensible to your poor, stunned date. Practice well before approaching them because scary as it sounds, you may not get another chance to woo them. Practice saying something passionate yet honest in front of the mirror to know

how you look and feel while saying it. See how your eyes look and pay close attention to your expressions.

2. Think carefully before you speak. Tide over a compelling feeling of nervousness before striking a conversation with your crush. Take a few minutes to think what and how you're going to approach them rather than thrusting yourself on their face like a bolt of lightning and talking rubbish. If the person is really important to you, it's worth it to take some time and then make a powerful first impression. Spontaneity is good, foolishness is not. Strike a fine balance between sounding like a well-rehearsed parrot and a totally unprepared clown.

3. Get to know them better. Your chances of success in asking your crush out for a date can be higher when you get to know them better. If you can, notice what they generally eat or what sport they're actively involved in or which team they support or even their favorite color. These details will give you a great ground for a later conversation. Something like, "You always carry these notebooks with iconic 90's movies. Is there a favorite you particularly enjoyed from that period?" See what you did? You were not in your face, but you kick-started a discussion that can open up so many conversational topics to cautiously test the waters.

4. Being independent of the outcome will increase your confidence. This has several advantages, though

it's easier said than done. It simply means you go into the scene of action without caring about the outcome. This will help you approach your date with greater confidence and cope with rejection more effectively. Try to think of it this way. Rejection simply means you're trying. And not getting rejected means you aren't trying enough. This approach will also allow you to enjoy a healthier camaraderie with your crush, irrespective of the outcome. Crushes aren't superheroes and your world doesn't crash if they reject you. They are special yes, but they are normal human beings.

5. Set the ground. When you come across your crush walking along alone, don't just grab the first opportunity to launch into verbal diarrhea about how much you adore them. Instead, use the opportunity to break the ice by just saying hi, and offering a warm and genuine smile if you don't know him/her too well. Next time you bump into them, strike when the iron is hot, and launch a conversation.

6. Your body language conveys things that remain unsaid. We've discussed earlier how body language can be a far more potent channel for communication than any verbal communication. Irrespective of what you say, if your body language is not in rhythm with what you are speaking, people immediately notice it. Make eye contact throughout the conversation. Smile. Face them directly. Don't fold your arms or play with

your hands/fingers. Keep your posture erect and the shoulders slightly tucked out. Lean a little forward when you're having a conversation to show you're genuinely interested in what they are saying.

7. Introduce yourself impressively. Don't get nervous and tongue-tied while introducing yourself. Emphasize on your name and say it clearly without stammering /stuttering (unless you have a genuine speech condition) or sounding awkward. The way you introduce yourself speaks volumes about your confidence and self-worth. It is a reflection of how you view yourself. Keep the tone of your voice friendly yet self-assured.

8. Do yourself a favor and avoid pick-up lines like the plague. Avoid using cheesy and hackneyed pickup lines that will have your crush scurrying in another direction unless you have something really smart and innovative to say. Nothing spells creep like an overused pickup line that's made only 'pick people up' so to speak.

9. Be yourself. As often as this is repeated, people still fail to understand its importance. You're definitely not setting the right ground for any budding relationship if it's based on a pretentious premise of who you really aren't. Keep your talk genuine, real, and personal. Don't pretend to be someone you clearly aren't. Know the fact that you are amazing as you are, and let that awesomeness reflect in your

conversation. If a person doesn't like you for who you truly are, ask yourself if it's an association worth pursuing.

10. Don't exaggerate or embellish while talking. Avoid overstating things just to find favor with your crush. They'll find us sooner or later and then all hell will break loose. If your crush says, he/she enjoys playing a sport, avoid declaring you have a keen interest in the game too when you don't. Their opinion of you will plummet once they discover the truth. You can be graceful and simply state that though you haven't had a chance to play it; you'd really love to give it a try. This way you're not dismissing it yet not actively professing to be a champ in it. You will come across as more genuine.

11. Break bad habits. If you have an overwhelmingly bad habit that keeps coming across when talking to your crush, you're at a huge disadvantage. Avoid cursing repetitively, calling everyone a fool, and talking non-stop of about how wonderful you are as a person. Try and keep the conversation clean, neutral, and positive. If being yourself means being ugly in your conversations, you might want to change yourself first.

12. Don't act overtly formal and scare them away. If you talk about taking them on a formal or elaborate date, chances are they'll break into a cold sweat. Rather, make it a friendly outing where you can head

to your nearest burger joint in jeans. It should be a more casual, friendly, and informal outing, like two friends getting to know each other, not a proper formal date, unless your crush wants it that way. There will be lesser pressure and a more relaxed atmosphere to break the ice.

13. Come to the point. After devoting enough occasions for small and ice, breakers, just go for the kill by asking direct. Don't sound phony and cheesy. Just appear confident, genuine, and friendly and don't try too hard. Simply ask them out for something harmless like a coffee, to begin with. Also, when you ask, be prepared to take no for answer. They may not have the same feelings as you do for them, and that's perfectly fine.

14. Handle rejection with grace. Don't throw tantrums or cry or walk off and create a scene. Appear strong and graceful when your crush rejects your request. Thank them graciously for considering it. For all you know, they might be impressed with your reaction or may just be testing you to check what you're really made of. They could be buying time and accessing you. Show your courageous side, know your self-worth, and walk away gracefully. You never know, you might just change their mind with your reaction. On the other hand, acting like a drama queen/king will convince them about how their decision to reject you was spot on. Avoid asking why

they made the decision they did. You're only digging for more dirt.

Chapter 4: 6 Social Skills That Can Change Your Life

Yes, life isn't fair. Some people are such naturals when it comes to talking to people in a relaxed, confident, and charming manner. However, acquiring social skills is no rocket science. It can be honed with training, practice, and conscious effort by just about anyone. It's never too late to start being the social champ you've always aspired to be. Mastering social skills training can be a brilliant boost to your self-confidence. Here are six vital social skills that can literally transform your life.

1. Listen to connect with people. Imagine you got on a date with a really hot looking guy. He's talented, looks divine and comes across as a really nice person. However, after the date is over, you're mighty glad it's over. Why? Because Mr. charming was only talking and talking and talking, without giving you an opportunity to respond or initiate a conversation. One of the most basic social skills that people still go completely wrong with is learning to listen. Communication is as much about listening as speaking, though some people consider only exceptional speaking skills as signs of good communication. Few things can be as appealing and likable as a person attentively listening to what you're saying. Learn to listen to people, and not just talk, to

build a connection. Listen, acknowledge, and respond with encouraging expressions/gestures.

2. Be in control of your emotions. Learn how not to be too agitated or anxious when around people, especially the ones you just can't stand. It impairs the functioning of the brain and doesn't allow us to think rationally. Be relaxed and calm in social situations. Don't let your body, expressions, and words give out that you're feeling strong emotions such as nervousness or anxiety from within. Learn how to keep a neutral and calm demeanor. It will help you connect with people more effectively. Controlling your emotions is a huge part of social skills training. Even when you disagree with people on controversial subjects, let them not get the better of you by turning you into a fuming moron. Be balanced yet assertive, rational, and polite while putting across your argument. You will earn more respect and people will actually listen to what you say.

3. Show empathy. Empathy is one of the most important social skills you can practice for leading a happy and successful life. You will attract greater personal and professional success when you learn to empathize with others. With empathy, you will learn to treat people in the exact manner in which you wish to be treated by them. You will be more in tune with their needs and understand them better. There will be a keen sense of understanding even what's been left

unsaid in your conversation with people. You will intuitively understand your colleagues, friends, customers, and family is developing a keen sense of empathy. There will be fewer conflicts in interpersonal relationships at work and at home. You will learn to correctly predict the actions people and learn to encourage those around you.

4. Doing self-disclosure the right way. Golden rule – A sure shot way to make people dislike you instantly is to talk a lot about yourself too early. Like we've seen earlier, good small talk is the one that doesn't comprise personal subjects. Stick to neutral subjects or exchange opinion in an objective manner. Don't go about revealing a lot about yourself or talk endlessly about topics personal to you when you don't know people well enough. You can't expect to share your innermost desires or darkest fears with a stranger without freaking them out. What and how much to disclose about yourself during different stages of interaction is a social art that's often neglected.

5. Eye contact and smile. If there are two magic weapons that can make you instantly attractive and likable to people, it's a genuine smile, followed by keen eye contact. It has been proved beyond doubt that looking into people's eyes and smiling is a brilliant way to establish an immediate liking and connection. Ever wondered, why you have an instant

and overpowering sense of like and dislike when you meet some people you know nothing about for the first time? It's the way they make an effort to connect with you through their eyes and smile, which convey more than words can. You will appear naturally attractive and desirable when you look directly at people and smile.

6. Rapport building. Good social interaction is all about building a strong connection with people. Unlike conversation, rapport building is more unconscious. It happens when your body language, speech, expressions, posture, and mannerisms match the other person. Though it is a highly unconscious process, it can be enhanced with social training. When you mirror and reflect people's actions, they are more likely to consider you as "one of them" and instantly establish a mental connection with you. Observe people closely. Mirror (and not mimic) their speech, words, and body language to build a rapport, naturally. This will also make you more outwardly focused and socially confident.

Chapter 5: 12 Powerful Rapport Building Secrets

Have you squirted oil into your vehicle's gears? Imagine them grinding together. The lubricating oil decreases friction and makes contact smoother. This is exactly how we interact with each other. Rapport is akin to the lubricating oil that helps reduce friction between two parties and paves the way for smoother communication. Rapport building is essential in every walk of life for everyone from a salesperson to a rock star to a CEO. Here are 10 powerful strategies for sharpening your rapport building skills.

1. Build on a Personal Connection

Build on similarities by establishing a common ground at the onset. It can be anything from being alumni from the same university to sharing similar hobbies to vacationing at a common destination. It is easier to develop both a personal and professional rapport with people who are similar to you.

Did you know that car salesmen are often trained to peep inside a prospective buyer's car and gather any clues to strike a conversation? If they spot a golf kit, they'll most likely throw in a bit about playing golf this weekend or if they find camping gear, they'll refer to their love for the outdoors subtly. The psychology behind this is that people instantly take to people who are like them or share their interests.

Intersecting with others on a common ground increases your chances of convincing or persuading others to your view or way. Quick words of caution – avoid controversial topics such as politics, religious faith, etc., and stick safe topics like sports and hobbies. Express an interest in causes that are close to the person's heart. Developing a greater sense of connection is integral to be an effective communicator.

2. Do a Little Digging Around

When you're going for an important meeting or even a first date, ensure you've done a little bit of research to create enough fodder for holding an arresting conversation. For instance, a person's social footprints (social media accounts) may indicate that he/she is heavily into charity and fundraising drives. This is your cue to learn about various fundraising drives and NGOs.

Even before heading to a party, gathering or business networking event, scan through the latest news or go through reviews of the most buzzing books/movies. This ensures you have plenty of conversation triggers that resonate with different groups of people.

3. Mix Statements with Questions

Make your rapport building small talk a mix of statements (mostly affirmative and positive) and questions. Don't ask questions that make the FBI seem like small players, and don't make to statements that don't give the other person an opportunity to talk.

Too much probing and people will feel like you're intruding their spread, too many statements and they'll feel like you don't really care about what they have to say. Something similar to, "though a lot of people hated it, I loved that reality television show, do you like it too?" You've stated your opinion, but you've also given the other person a chance to share his/her views.

Have you heard of the term quid pro quo? It simply means giving something to get something in return. In conversation and rapport building it means you share something about yourself to get the other person to share something about himself. It is similar to conversation bait that is aimed at drawing the other person into an engaging conversation.

4. Make a Grand Entry

No, I am not talking a Hollywood-risqué James Bond entry but one that helps people notice you as a confident, charismatic person as soon as you enter. Avoid looking at the floor or ceiling while entering. Keep your back and head straight up. Don't slouch.

Pull back your shoulders and leave your hands loosely on the sides.

To make an even more impactful entry, walk in with someone by your side. It can be anyone from your co-worker to a friend to a sibling. It throws more glances your way.

5. Be Your Real Self

As many times as this golden piece of wisdom is reiterated in self-help groups, people still find it tough to understand the importance of being yourself. If you start by building a rapport/relationship on a fake premise, it's guaranteed to collapse someday. Keep your introduction, self-talk, and other communication genuine and personal.

Don't feign to be someone other than what you truly are. Of course, constantly developing/improving your persona is one thing, and pretending to be someone else completely another. If you have to be someone else, the association you're pursuing may not be worth it.

People are attracted to real, warm, and effervescent folks who appear happy, friendly and bubbly. It will make your instantly likable, while also helping those who are anxious around you relax a bit.

6. Killer Conversation Starters

Whether you are seeking to develop rapport personally or professionally, there are some conversation starters that rarely go wrong. They entice people into an interesting conversation and make you come across as a master communicator. Here are a few examples for you to try on your next rapport building adventure.

How was the weekend? Did you do something interesting?

Pay a sincere compliment, and then ask the other person an open-ended question about the thing you've just complimented them on. For instance, "I really love the artwork on the lobby walls, where did you source it from?"

Ask for suggestions/guidance or positioning other people as an expert is another strategy that works wonders when it comes to rapport building. For instance, "Are you from New York City? Can you suggest some cool underground bars here for a first-timer like me?"

You can also be the guide by inquiring by welcoming a new person to your town/city, and inquiring, have you been to NYC before? Where are you put up? Isn't the city dramatically different from London?" You're drawing the person into a conversation by positioning yourself as an expert, while also letting them express their opinion.

7. Be Culturally Sensitive

Yes, the world has become a global village, and people from multiple cultures interact with each other. There's no need to bend backward to please people from other cultures and forget where you're from.

However, it is also important to be sensitive to other cultures by updating yourself about the norms and patterns of various cultures. It gives you a firm ground to establish your communication style. Something that's considered acceptable in one culture may be totally inappropriate in another.

For example, in the US, a brief and firm handshake is a sign of confidence and strength, while a lame handshake is seen as a sign of weakness. However, in several African regions, people look up to a limp and long handshake as appropriate. A lingering handshake is considered a sign of familiarity and sexual attraction in the US.

8. Match Energy Levels

Closely observe the energy levels of the person you are communicating with and try to match it. Is the person more shy, reticent, and withdrawn? Is he/she more gregarious and exuberant? Of course, you don't have to undergo a personality transformation. All you need to do is try to communicate with people with similar energy levels to make the process more effective.

For instance, if the other person is timid and reserved in demeanor, and if you talk nineteen to the dozen, you may unknowingly come across as aggressive and intimidating. Similarly, match the other person's voice tone too. Being loud when the other person is speaking in a softer tone will not help you break the ice with the other person. The idea is to be on the same plane in terms of energy and speech tone.

Practicing matching the depth or tone of people's voice isn't tough. People either talk predominantly through their throat (much like Kermit the Frog), nose (sounds more congested) or chest (deep loud voice). Keep shuffling the depth of your voice periodically to match other people to resonate with them.

9. What's in It for Them?

This is especially true when you are trying to build a rapport with people professionally but also works well on the personal front. Rather than focusing on what you have to offer or how it impacts you, tell the person what's in it for him/her.

People focus too much on waxing eloquence about the features of their products or themselves (think how to sell yourself on a first date). Mention the benefits or what the other person stands to gain.

One of the biggest reasons why several salespersons fail to meet their sales quotas is because they are selling rather than helping the customer buy. When you help them buy, they're sold? Think from the perspective of the other person as a communicator. How will a certain product or service affect them? How will it make their life easier? What will then gain a result of buying your product or service? Structure your pitch around how the product or service will add value to their life.

10. Maintain Eye Contact

One of the easiest and sure-shot ways to let people know you are interested in what they are saying is by maintaining eye contact. If you are looking all around the place, you appear distracted and disinterested. It makes the other person feel less valued. Of course, you have to gaze in another direction for a few seconds in between or they'll get the impression you're staring at them or trying to intimidate them.

This is a universal rapport building trick that makes you instantly likable to people across multiple cultures. Giving people undivided and undistracted attention when they are speaking is one of the biggest signs of a master communicator. Contrary to what people believe, communication is as much about listening effectively as it's about speaking effectively. Maintaining eye contact for a major part of the conversation spells confidence and attentiveness, which increases your likeability quotient.

11. Own Your Reactions

You often hear people say, "He/she-she made me feel terrible about myself" or "I had no option but to react the way I did." There may not be many lucrative choices but being in control of your reactions or owning your reactions makes you a master communicator who has the ability to persuade and influence people.

There's no need to defend yourself all the time or debate what the other person is saying. Weigh your reactions carefully and speak slowly yet assertively rather than displaying irrational reactions (screaming or giving lengthy explanations). Make your point firmly but don't let your voice show visible signs of emotions. Use the compare and contrast technique here too. For example, "

It makes you come across a more authoritative and in control person who leaves no scope for miscommunication. For instance, "contrary to what you believe, I listen to you otherwise I wouldn't have called the electrician on time as you instructed me to." Also, I wouldn't have filed the papers in order as requested by you."

Asking for clarifications if you haven't understood what the other person is saying is always a good practice. The best way to accomplish this is by paraphrasing what you just heard. For instance, "If I understand correctly, what you said is xyz." Paraphrasing your understanding of the other person's words eliminates the scope for further misunderstanding.

Rather than losing your cool, calmly list all the instances where you have done something contrary to what the other person is pulling you up for. This minimizes the scope for further miscommunication, hostility, and accusations.

Also, when it's genuinely your mistake, owning up makes you come across as a stronger person. Don't try to duck the blame or make someone else the scapegoat. Accept you goofed up rather than coming across as a wimp, and say you'll be more mindful about not repeating the mistake in future.

People who drown their egos and accept responsibility for their acts are charismatic communicators who lead by example.

Play the unifying mediator if you really want to be recognized as a master communicator. When discussions and negotiations drag forever, are proactive and take control of things by acting as an effective mediator. If you step in and resolve the issue, people will almost always remember you as a charismatic peacemaker. Be the unifying force that calms down the situation assertively. Make your point gently and effectively and establish a middle line that resonates with both parties.

12. Agree with People's Emotions

You may not always agree with people's opinions or "facts" stated by them. However, there's no stopping you from agreeing with their emotions. When you agree with people emotionally, it almost always helps you make a powerful connection with them.

For example, you can say, "You sound bitter. That must've hurt a lot" or "I really can't blame you for sounding --------." It can also be something like, "I'd be upset too if this happened with me" or I am sorry you are feeling this way or you have to go through this" or "I understand how terrible it is."

This almost always works wonders because unlike facts, feelings aren't correct or incorrect." There's nothing right or wrong about emotions, which is why it is easy to make someone feel like you're with them on how they are feeling.

Conclusion

Thank you for downloading this book.

I sincerely hope it has given you multiple strategies, actionable tips and proven techniques for being a social champ across multiple settings to enjoy more balanced, rewarding and fulfilling social, professional, and personal relationships.

The objective of the book is to help you eliminate inhibitions, anxiety, nervousness, and lack of confidence to take on the world by speaking more confidently, persuasively and effectively, conquering one skill at a time until you can speak to anyone like a charmer. Communication and conversation are the key towards building strong, rewarding, and enduring relationships along with impacting your chances of success in life.

The next step is to start using all the pointers mentioned in the book immediately. The information has to be converted into knowledge, which in turn is translated into experience and wisdom. Of course, you won't transform from a greenhorn conversationalist or social being into a social ninja overnight. Rome wasn't built in a day. However, one step a time you'll get closer to your goal. With application and practice, you'll slowly but surely transform into an interesting, engaging, and stimulating conversationalist.

!A information can be obtained
w.ICGtesting.com
⁴ in the USA
⁷031402180719
'39BV00001B/44/P

9 781646 156092

FREE BONUS

P.S. Is it okay if we overdeliver?

I believe in overdelivering way beyond our reader's expectations. Is it okay if I overdeliver?

Here's the deal, I am going to give you an extremely valuable cheatsheet of "Accelerated Learning"...

What's the catch? I need to trust you... You see, my team and I wants to overdeliver and in order for us to do that, we've to trust our reader to keep this bonus a secret to themselves. Why? Because we don't want people to be getting our ultimate accelerated learning cheatsheet without even buying our books itself. Unethical, right?

Ok. Are you ready?

Simply   Visit   this
http://bit.ly/acceleratedcheatsheet

Everything else will be self explanatory
visited: http://bit.ly/acceleratedche

We hope you'll enjoy our free b
we've enjoyed preparing it for yo